100 facts

SPACE TRAVEL

100 facts

SPACE TRAVEL

Sue Becklake

Consultant: Clive Gifford

Miles Kelly

First published in 2015 by Miles Kelly Publishing Ltd
Harding's Barn, Bardfield End Green, Thaxted, Essex, CM6 3PX, UK

Copyright © Miles Kelly Publishing Ltd 2015

This edition printed 2018

4 6 8 10 9 7 5 3

PUBLISHING DIRECTOR Belinda Gallagher
CREATIVE DIRECTOR Jo Cowan
EDITORIAL DIRECTOR Rosie Neave
EDITORS Sarah Parkin, Amy Johnson
DESIGNERS D&A Design, Joe Jones
IMAGE MANAGER Liberty Newton
INDEXER Jane Parker
PRODUCTION Elizabeth Collins, Jennifer Brunwin-Jones
REPROGRAPHICS Stephan Davis, Jennifer Cozens, Thom Allaway
ASSETS Lorraine King

ISBN 978-1-78209-647-4

Printed in China

British Library Cataloguing-in-Publication Data
A catalogue record for this book is available from the British Library

ACKNOWLEDGEMENTS
The publishers would like to thank the following artists who have contributed to this book:
Peter Bull, Mike Foster (Maltings Partnership)
All other artwork from the Miles Kelly Artwork Bank

The publishers would like to thank the following sources for the use of their photographs:
Key: t = top, b = bottom, l = left, r = right, c = centre, m= main, bg = background, rt = repeated throughout
Cover: (front) Dennis Hallinan/Alamy, (back, t) NASA/ESA/Alexander Gerst

Corbis 9(m) Scott Andrews/Science Faction; 15(tr) Alexander Nemenov/epa; 16–17(m) Roger Ressmeyer; 31(r) and 39(b) Victor
Habbick Visions/Science Photo Library **NASA** 2–3; 5(tr) NASA Headquarters – GReatest Images of NASA (NASA-HQ-GRIN); 6–7;
8(panel, b); 18(tr) Great Images in NASA (NASA-GRIN); 24(m) NASA-GRIN; 28(bl) NASA-GRIN; 32(tl); 33(bl); 34–35(m) NASA-
GRIN; 41(tl) **Rex Features** 20(tl) Everett Collection, (tr); 30(b); 31(cl) Snap Stills; 45(br) c.20thC.Fox/Everett; 46–47(m) Paramount
Pictures/courtesy Everett Collection; 47(br) c.Universal/Everett **Science Photo Library** 11(t) David Ducros, ESA; 13(br) NASA;
14–15(m) NASA; 14(tr); 18(m) Alexis Rosenfeld; 19(b, bg) NASA; 25(m) NASA; 30(t) NASA; 33(r) Detlev van Ravenswaay;
36(tr) Roger Harris, (c) David Ducros; 37(t) Friedrich Saurer, (br) Ton Kinsbergen; 38(m) Carlos Clarivan; 39(tl) David A. Hardy,
Futures: 50 Years in Space; 40(m) David Ducros; 41(b) David Parker, (br) European Space Agency; 42–43(m) Detlev van
Ravenswaay; 44–45(m) David A. Hardy, Futures: 50 Years in Space; 45(tr) Henning Dalhoff **Shutterstock.com** 8(bl, bg) J. Helgason,
(panel, t) Rob Wilson, (panel, c) DenisKlimov, (br, bg, rt) Stephen Rees; 9(quiz panel, rt) caesart, (br, bg) NRT;
11(activity panel, rt) Shawn Hine; 12(bl, bg) STILLFX; 13(IDBI panel, rt) fluidworkshop; 28–29(bg) R-studio; 29(t, bg) Aleksandr
Bryliaev; 30–31(bg) Procy; 34(bl, bg) Jozef Sowa; 35(cr, bg) cluckva, (bl, bg) Baloncici; 38(bl, bg); 40(br, bg) nuttakit;
41(br, bg) Petrov Stanislav; 42(bl, bg) FotograFFF; 43(br, bg) lukeruk; 46(bl, bg) ninanaina, (br, bg) Stephen Rees
Topfoto 25(t) United Archives

All other photographs are from:
digitalSTOCK, digitalvision, John Foxx, PhotoAlto, PhotoDisc, PhotoEssentials, PhotoPro, Stockbyte

Every effort has been made to acknowledge the source and copyright holder of each picture.
Miles Kelly Publishing apologizes for any unintentional errors or omissions.

Made with paper from a sustainable forest

www.mileskelly.net

The publishers would like to thank the Society for Popular Astronomy for their help in compiling this book.

CONTENTS

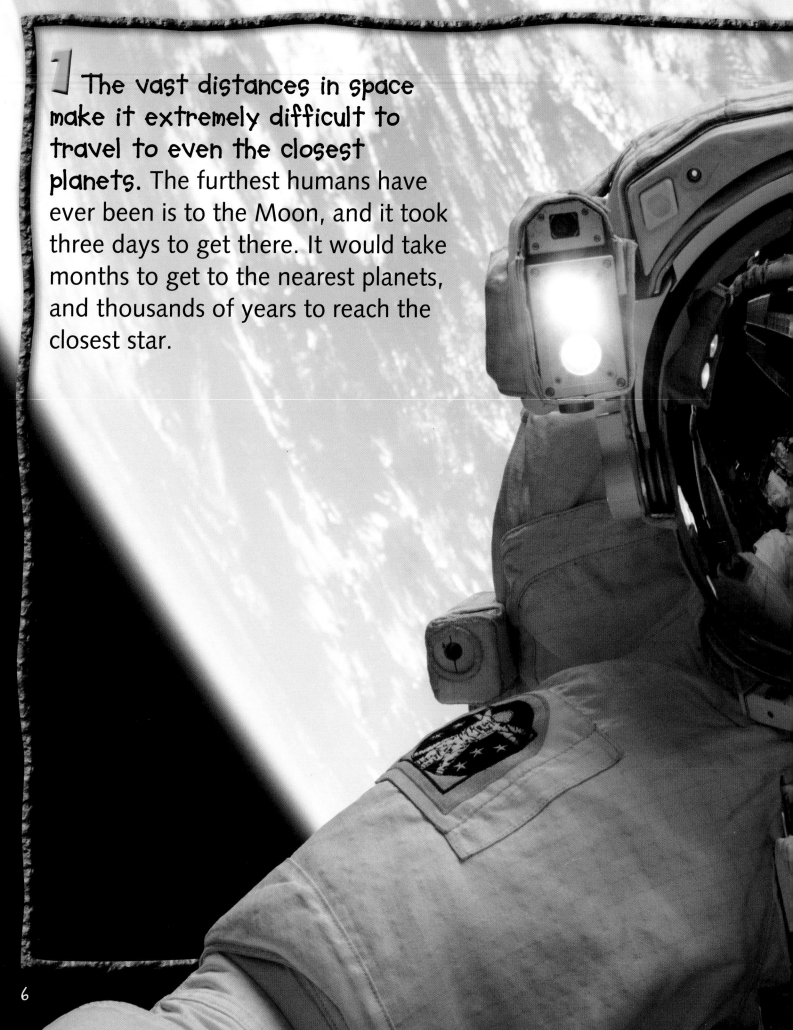

Travelling in space

1 The vast distances in space make it extremely difficult to travel to even the closest planets. The furthest humans have ever been is to the Moon, and it took three days to get there. It would take months to get to the nearest planets, and thousands of years to reach the closest star.

◄ Astronauts can now live in space, in the orbiting International Space Station, seen here reflected in the visor of NASA astronaut Mike Hopkins' spacesuit.

Escape from Earth

2 **Gravity is the force that pulls everything down towards Earth.** All objects are pulled towards each other by gravity, but bigger things have a stronger pull. Earth is huge, and so pulls everything smaller towards it. This is why you don't float away, and why it is difficult to travel into space.

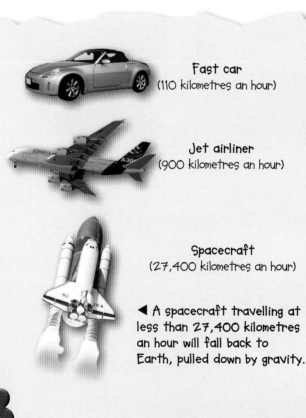

Fast car
(110 kilometres an hour)

Jet airliner
(900 kilometres an hour)

Spacecraft
(27,400 kilometres an hour)

◀ A spacecraft travelling at less than 27,400 kilometres an hour will fall back to Earth, pulled down by gravity.

3 **The way to overcome this pull of gravity and reach space is to travel very fast.** A spacecraft must get up to a speed of about 27,400 kilometres an hour. This is about 30 times faster than a cruising jet airliner, and 250 times faster than a car travelling on a motorway.

4 **Even 27,400 kilometres an hour is not fast enough for a spacecraft to break free of Earth's gravity.** At this speed it will circle round Earth about 200 kilometres above the ground – it is in orbit. Spacecraft orbit at different speeds depending on their distance from Earth – the pull of gravity decreases the further you are from Earth.

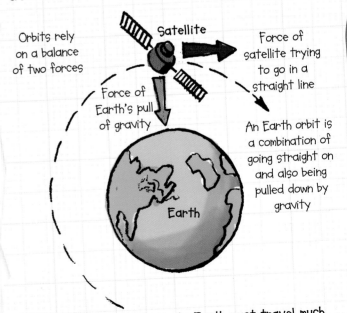

Orbits rely on a balance of two forces

Satellite

Force of satellite trying to go in a straight line

Force of Earth's pull of gravity

An Earth orbit is a combination of going straight on and also being pulled down by gravity

Earth

▲ Satellites orbiting closer to Earth must travel much faster than those in higher orbits.

► An Atlas rocket gave the *New Horizons* space probe the fastest ever launch speed for its journey to distant Pluto.

5 Spacecraft need even more speed to escape from the pull of Earth's gravity completely and fly off into space. They have to travel at 40,000 kilometres an hour – this speed is called Earth's escape velocity. Once in space there is no air to slow a spacecraft down, so it doesn't need powerful engines to keep going.

QUIZ

1. How fast is Earth's escape velocity?
2. How far away is the nearest star from the Sun?
3. What is the name of the force that stops you just floating away from Earth?

Answers:
1. 40,000 kilometres an hour
2. 4.2 light-years (40 million million kilometres) 3. Gravity

6 Distances in space are vast – so huge that astronomers do not use kilometres or miles to measure them. One measure of distance is the light-year, which is the distance that light travels in one year, and is equal to 9.46 million million kilometres. The nearest star to the Sun is 4.2 light-years away – equivalent to nearly 40 million million kilometres.

Light takes 8 minutes to reach Earth from the Sun

Sun

Earth

▲ A car travelling at 60 kilometres an hour would take 285 years to get to the Sun.

Rocket power

7 Rocket engines provide the enormous power needed to launch a spacecraft with enough speed to fly into space. On Earth, engines use oxygen from the air to burn their fuel, but in space there is no air to provide oxygen. Rocket engines can work in space because they have their own supply of oxygen gas.

8 Inside a rocket engine, fuel is burnt to make hot gases. The gases shoot out of a nozzle at the back of the rocket, pushing it forwards at high speed. Some rockets use a liquid fuel, which is pumped into the engine where it is mixed with oxygen and burnt. Other rockets use solid fuel – a rubbery material containing oxygen.

Key
1. Satellite payload
2. Second stage
3. First stage
4. Liquid oxygen tank
5. Liquid hydrogen fuel tank
6. Booster rocket
7. Solid fuel
8. First stage engine

▶ An Ariane 5 rocket has two stages and two solid rocket boosters to launch satellites into orbit.

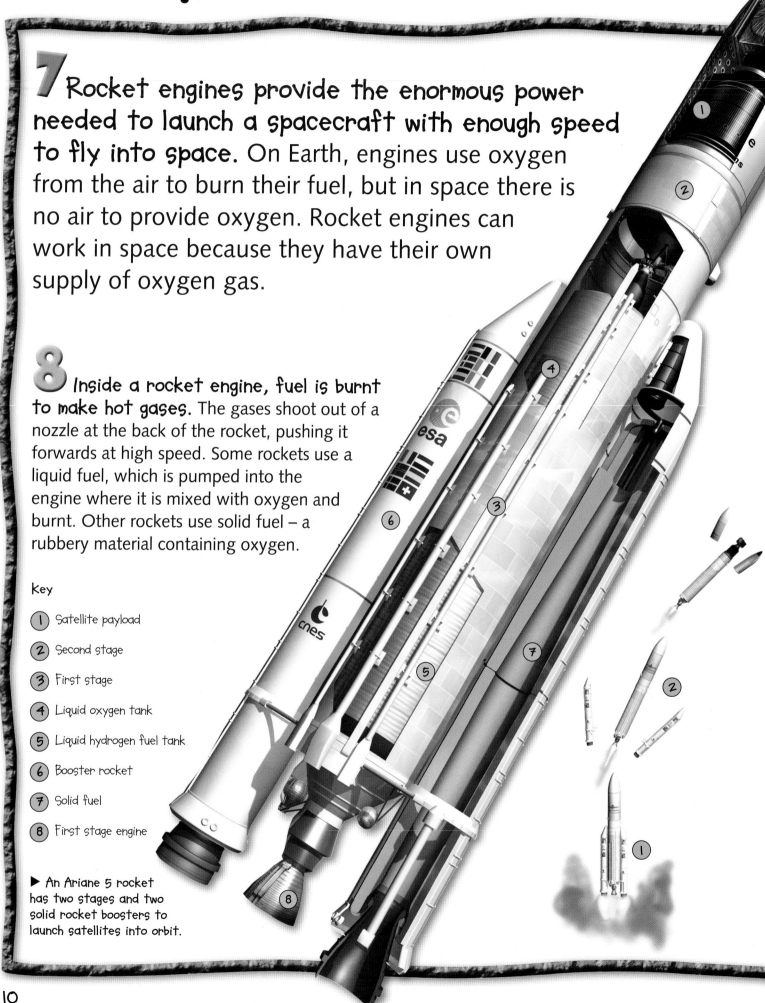

9 Booster rockets can supply extra power for a launch. These are separate rockets strapped to the side of the main rocket. They burn their fuel then break away and fall back to Earth. The space shuttle used two huge booster rockets, and the Russian Soyuz rockets have four boosters strapped around them at take-off.

► Ariane 5 boosters burn their fuel in about two minutes then fall away into the sea.

▲ Ariane 5 launch: Lift-off (1), boosters fall away (2), first stage separates (3), second stage puts satellite into orbit (4).

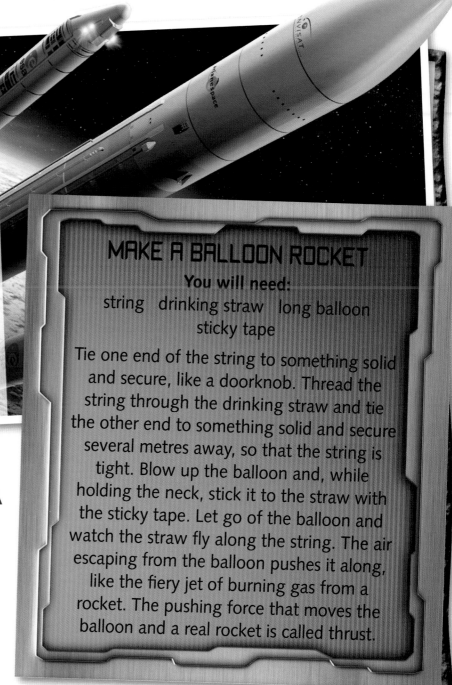

MAKE A BALLOON ROCKET
You will need:
string   drinking straw   long balloon
sticky tape

Tie one end of the string to something solid and secure, like a doorknob. Thread the string through the drinking straw and tie the other end to something solid and secure several metres away, so that the string is tight. Blow up the balloon and, while holding the neck, stick it to the straw with the sticky tape. Let go of the balloon and watch the straw fly along the string. The air escaping from the balloon pushes it along, like the fiery jet of burning gas from a rocket. The pushing force that moves the balloon and a real rocket is called thrust.

10 Several rocket stages are needed to reach space. Each stage has its own engine and fuel. The first stage lifts the rocket and spacecraft off the ground. When it has used up its fuel, it separates from the rest of the rocket and falls back to Earth. The next stage engine starts up, giving the rocket extra speed. It then falls away and the third stage takes the spacecraft into orbit.

11 New space planes are being designed that may make it easier and cheaper to fly into space. One is called *Skylon*. It will have engines that can use oxygen gas from the air until it reaches space. This means it will be lighter and need less power to take off because it will carry less oxygen. *Skylon* will take off and land on a runway and will be able to fly many times.

Space shuttle

12 Most rockets can only be launched once, but the space shuttle was a reusable spaceplane with rocket engines. It had three main parts: an orbiter, a huge fuel tank and two giant boosters. Only the orbiter went into space. Five orbiters were built – *Columbia*, *Challenger*, *Discovery*, *Atlantis* and *Endeavour* – and each flew in space many times.

▶ At lift-off the enormous tank supplied the shuttle's three main engines with fuel. While the shuttle was attached to the tank during lift-off, its cargo bay doors were shut. The doors only opened when the shuttle reached orbit.

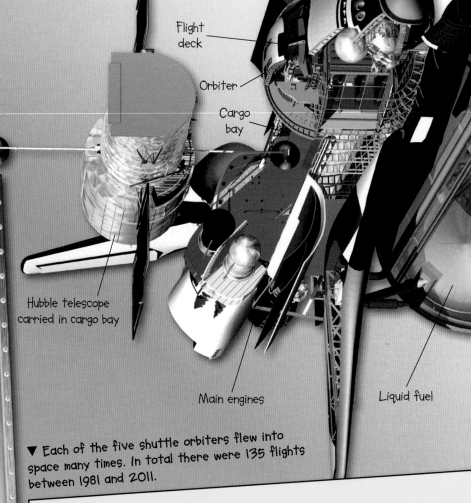

Cargo bay door

Flight deck

Orbiter

Cargo bay

Hubble telescope carried in cargo bay

Main engines

Liquid fuel

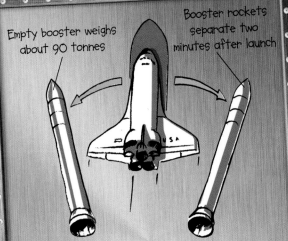

Empty booster weighs about 90 tonnes

Booster rockets separate two minutes after launch

13 The shuttle took off upwards like a rocket. The orbiter's three rocket engines and two huge booster rockets all fired together at launch. The solid fuel in the boosters only took two minutes to burn up, then they fell away into the sea.

▼ Each of the five shuttle orbiters flew into space many times. In total there were 135 flights between 1981 and 2011.

🚀 Shuttle flights

Orbiter	First flight	Last flight	No. of flights
Columbia	12 April, 1981	16 Jan, 2003	28
Challenger	4 April, 1983	28 Jan, 1986	10
Discovery	30 Aug, 1984	24 Feb, 2011	39
Atlantis	3 Oct, 1985	8 July, 2011	33
Endeavour	7 May, 1992	16 May, 2011	25

Fuel
tank

Double-skin
tank walls

14 The shuttle orbiter could carry seven astronauts into space. They lived and worked in the cabin at the front of the orbiter on missions lasting one to two weeks at a time.

15 Satellites were launched from the shuttle's cargo bay. The shuttle placed the Hubble Space Telescope into orbit, and there were five later shuttle missions to repair it in space. On other flights the cargo bay held a laboratory called Spacelab where the astronauts carried out experiments.

Boosters

16 The shuttle orbiters carried many of the International Space Station's parts into space. Space station modules where the astronauts would live and work fitted into the shuttle's cargo bay for the journey. Each part was added to the space station by spacewalking astronauts, who gradually built it while it orbited Earth.

▼ Space shuttle *Atlantis* docked with the ISS during the shuttle's final mission in July 2011.

13

Returning to Earth

17 One of the most dangerous parts of space travel is re-entry (returning to Earth's atmosphere). When spacecraft come back they rub against the air at incredible speeds, which makes them extremely hot. The space shuttle reached temperatures of about 1650°C on re-entry.

▲ The shuttle glowed red hot when re-entering Earth's atmosphere. To avoid burning up, spacecraft must re-enter at exactly the right angle.

18 Astronauts in a returning spacecraft are protected from the heat by a heat shield. On the space shuttle the heat shield was made of special tiles that covered the shuttle's underside. These stopped the heat from reaching the rest of the shuttle. Other spacecraft like the Russian Soyuz are protected by thick material that burns away but keeps the spacecraft cool.

19 The shuttle landed on a runway like an aircraft, but without using its engines, more like a huge glider. It travelled halfway round the world to its landing site, gliding through the air and slowing down by turning left and right. It came to a stop on the runway by using parachutes and brakes on its landing wheels to slow it. After servicing, the orbiter could be launched into space again.

▼ A Soyuz space capsule carrying three cosmonauts home from the *Mir* space station throws up dust as it lands in a desert area.

◄ The space shuttle needed a very long runway to land safely at the end of a mission.

20 The Soyuz spacecraft uses parachutes to slow it down as it falls through the air. Just before it hits the ground, small rocket motors fire to slow it even more and give it a soft landing. Some early spacecraft, like the Command Modules from the Apollo missions to the Moon, came down to Earth by parachute before splashing into the sea for a soft landing.

FEEL THE HEAT OF FRICTION
Rub your hands together or rub them against your legs. Do they start to feel warm? This is the way a spacecraft heats up when it rubs against the air. A force called friction makes the heat by trying to stop the rubbing movement. You can even start a fire using friction by rubbing two dry sticks together.

Spacecraft

21 Spacecraft are vehicles that travel to destinations in space. Some are built to carry people on board, but these do not travel far from Earth. Unmanned spacecraft can travel much further. People have sent unmanned spacecraft to all the other planets orbiting the Sun, and some space probes and rovers have even landed on some of them. Several have flown beyond the furthest planet in our Solar System, out towards the distant stars.

▶ The *Galileo* space probe orbited the giant planet Jupiter and dropped a smaller probe into Jupiter's bright clouds.

22 With no air to push against, a spacecraft will keep going steadily through space. However, spacecraft have engines to change direction and keep them on course, and to slow them down when they get to their destination. The engines can also provide extra speed to make the journey quicker. The spacecraft must carry all the fuel its engines need for the whole journey.

23 All spacecraft need power to operate and to keep warm — it is extremely cold in space. Solar panels that change sunlight into electricity can provide enough power for spacecraft close to the Sun. Those that travel far away from the Sun often use nuclear power. The space shuttle had fuel cells that made electricity by turning oxygen and hydrogen into water.

24 Spacecraft send back information and receive instructions from controllers on Earth using radio signals. As a spacecraft travels further away the radio signals get weaker. Probes going to distant planets need large dish-shaped antennae (aerials) to send and receive messages. Back on Earth, huge receivers collect the faint signals.

I DON'T BELIEVE IT!

UFOs (Unidentified Flying Objects) are objects in the sky that do not look like ordinary planes. Some people think that UFOs are alien spacecraft from other stars or planets visiting Earth, but there is no evidence for this.

25 Manned spacecraft must be able to keep the astronauts inside alive and well. They are built with a strong double outer layer to protect the crew from dangerous radiation and speeding space dust. They contain a supply of air to breathe and enough water and food for the whole journey. The temperature is kept comfortable using radiators to lose excess heat into space.

Astronauts

26 People who travel in space are called astronauts. In Russia they are called cosmonauts and in China they are called taikonauts. Astronauts from many different countries have gone into space, most of them in Russian and US spacecraft. So far, the only country other than Russia and the US to have launched astronauts into space is China.

▲ Trainee astronauts float inside an aircraft as if they are in space.

▶ ESA (European Space Agency) astronaut Jean-Francois Clervoy trains for spacewalks wearing a spacesuit underwater.

27 Astronauts need many months of training to get them ready for a spaceflight. They learn about the spacecraft they will be living and working in, and what to do in an emergency. Astronauts train in huge tanks of water to get used to the feeling of weightlessness and practise for spacewalks outside the spacecraft.

QUIZ

1. What are Chinese astronauts called?
2. How long do astronauts exercise for each day?
3. Why do astronauts train in huge tanks of water?

Answers:
1. Taikonauts 2. About two hours 3. To get used to the feeling of weightlessness

28 It is essential for astronauts to be fit and healthy. Before they fly there are many medical checks to make sure they will not fall ill in space. In their spacecraft they exercise regularly, usually for about two hours a day by using an exercise bike, running on a treadmill or doing a space version of weightlifting. This helps to keep their muscles and bones strong.

29 Living in space for a long time can make your muscles weaker and your body slightly taller. When floating in a spacecraft, you do not use the muscles that normally keep you standing up. The bones that make up your spine aren't squashed together by gravity, and so they stretch apart. Astronauts soon return to normal back on Earth.

30 Astronauts have many different jobs in space. Some are trained as pilots to fly the spacecraft. Others go outside the spacecraft or space station, where they carry out spacewalks to install equipment or do repairs. Inside, they perform experiments to explore the effects of space travel.

Key

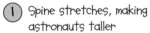

(1) Spine stretches, making astronauts taller

(2) Leg and back muscles weaken

(3) Leg and back bones get weaker and thinner

(4) Face becomes puffy

▼ In space, gravity does not pull down on an astronaut's body.

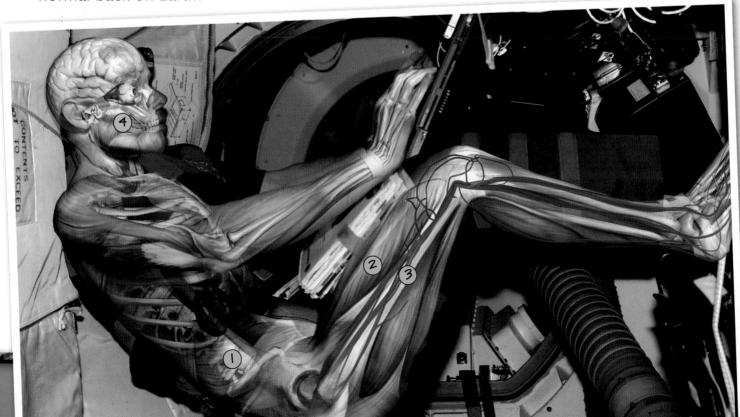

Space pioneers

31 The first person to fly into space was a Russian called Yuri Gagarin. On 12 April, 1961 he completed one orbit round Earth in his spacecraft *Vostok 1*. Soon after Gagarin's flight, on 5 May, 1961, Alan Shepherd became the first American in space, although he didn't orbit Earth.

▲ Yuri Gagarin's historic flight lasted 1 hour and 48 minutes.

32 Two years after Gagarin's flight, on 16 June, 1963, Valentina Tereshkova became the **first woman in space.** She spent nearly three days in orbit, circling Earth 48 times during her flight in the *Vostok 6* spacecraft.

▲ Valentina Tereshkova was only 26 when she flew in space.

33 The first person to leave a spacecraft and go on a spacewalk was a Russian called Alexei Leonov, on 18 March, 1965. He was out in space for 12 minutes attached to his spacecraft by a tether to stop him floating away.

▲ Alexei Leonov left his *Voskhod* spacecraft through an airlock to perform the extremely dangerous spacewalk.

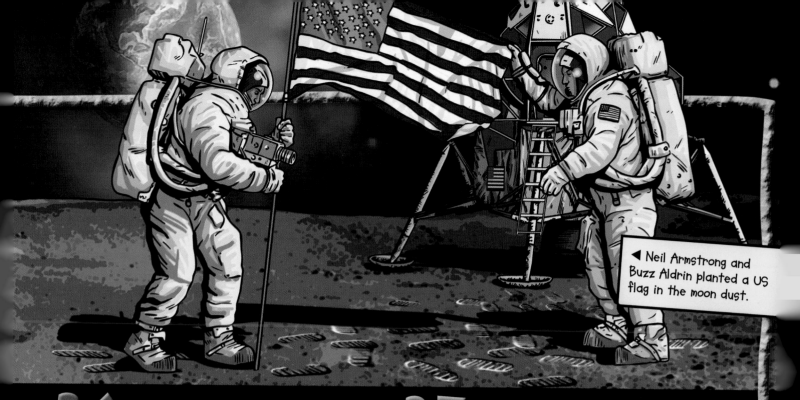

◄ Neil Armstrong and Buzz Aldrin planted a US flag in the moon dust.

34
The first Moon landing took place on 20 July, 1969. Two American astronauts landed the *Apollo 11* lunar lander in an area of the Moon called the Sea of Tranquillity. Neil Armstrong was the first to set foot on the surface, followed by Buzz Aldrin. They spent about two and a half hours outside on the surface, exploring and collecting rocks to take back to Earth.

35
Since these early pioneers, several astronauts have spent over a year in space. Valeri Polyakov stayed aboard the *Mir* space station for nearly 438 days (about 14 months) in 1994 to 1995. Others have only spent longer in space if you add together all their different space flights. Sergei Krikalev has had six flights totalling over 800 days (over two years).

SPACE TIMELINE

4 October, 1957
The first artificial satellite, *Sputnik 1*, was launched.

→

3 November, 1957
A dog called Laika became the first animal in space.

→

12 April, 1961
The first human, Yuri Gagarin, was launched into space.

20 July, 1969
The first manned spacecraft landed on the Moon, and Neil Armstrong became the first person to walk on the surface.

←

18 March, 1965
Alexei Leonov was the first person to leave a spacecraft and 'walk' in space.

←

16 June, 1963
Valentina Tereshkova became the first woman in space.

19 April, 1971
The first space station, *Salyut 1*, was launched into orbit.

→

14 December, 1972
Apollo 17, the last manned mission to the Moon, left the Moon.

→

12 April, 1981
The first flight of the re-useable space shuttle.

→

20 February, 1986
The first module of the *Mir* space station was launched, with other modules and equipment added over the next 10 years.

31 October, 2000
The first crew visited the ISS.

←

20 November, 1998
The first module of the International Space Station (ISS), Zarya, was launched.

←

22 March, 1995
Valeri Polyakov set the record for the longest single spaceflight.

Spacesuits

36 Astronauts could not survive outside their spacecraft without a spacesuit. They put it on inside an airlock (airtight chamber) which has two doors, one opening into the spacecraft and the other to the outside. Once inside their suit they close the inner door, let the air out of the airlock, open the outer door and go outside.

37 Spacesuits are very bulky because they have to keep astronauts alive and protect them from speeding space dust. They are made of many different layers of material – 14 for a NASA spacesuit. The outer layers are waterproof, fireproof and bulletproof. Underneath are insulating layers that keep the temperature steady and a rip-proof layer that stops the suit from tearing.

38 The spacesuit must press down on an astronaut's body. Without this pressure their bodies would swell and gases would bubble out of their blood like boiling water. On Earth the air is always pressing down on our bodies, but in space there is no air. In a spacesuit the pressure comes from a double layer blown up like a balloon, in the shape of a human body.

Key
1. Lights
2. Helmet
3. Visor
4. Gloves
5. Control panel
6. Tether
7. Backpack with life support system
8. Boots

▲ Spacesuits provide a life-support system for astronauts while outside the spacecraft.

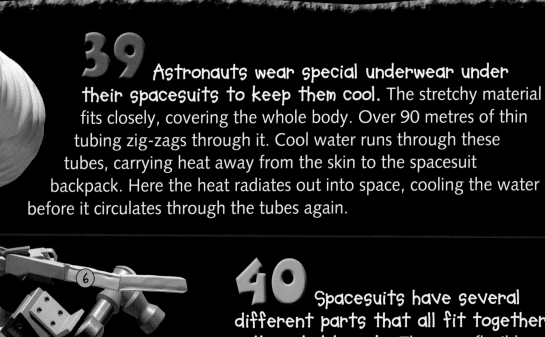

39 Astronauts wear special underwear under their spacesuits to keep them cool. The stretchy material fits closely, covering the whole body. Over 90 metres of thin tubing zig-zags through it. Cool water runs through these tubes, carrying heat away from the skin to the spacesuit backpack. Here the heat radiates out into space, cooling the water before it circulates through the tubes again.

40 Spacesuits have several different parts that all fit together with airtight seals. There are flexible joints in the shoulders, arms and wrists so that the astronauts can move their hands and arms to work in space. The helmet over the head is made of tough clear plastic to give the astronaut a good view. Under the helmet, a cap with a radio lets the astronaut talk to other astronauts or ground control.

I DON'T BELIEVE IT!

The NASA spacesuits that the astronauts wear on spacewalks at the ISS cost $12 million each. Astronauts do not have their own individual spacesuits. The parts come in different sizes so each astronaut can put together a spacesuit that fits him or her.

Spacewalks

41 Extravehicular Activity (EVA), often called a spacewalk, is when an astronaut leaves the spacecraft to work outside in space. They might be building or repairing a space station, or servicing satellites. Experiments that need to be exposed directly to space are fixed to the outside of a spacecraft and collected during spacewalks.

◀ This astronaut is working without a tether. He is wearing a SAFER (Simplified Aid for EVA Rescue) backpack. It can be controlled by small jets of nitrogen, which allow the astronaut to fly back to the space station.

42 A safety tether stops astronauts from floating away from their spacecraft. It is like a rope with one end fixed to the spacecraft and the other to the spacesuit. Tools used by the astronauts are also tethered to the spacesuit so they don't get lost in space.

I DON'T BELIEVE IT!
Spacewalking astronauts may have to stay in their spacesuits for up to eight hours without a toilet break. They wear a Maximum Absorption Garment (MAG) under their spacesuit to absorb the waste.

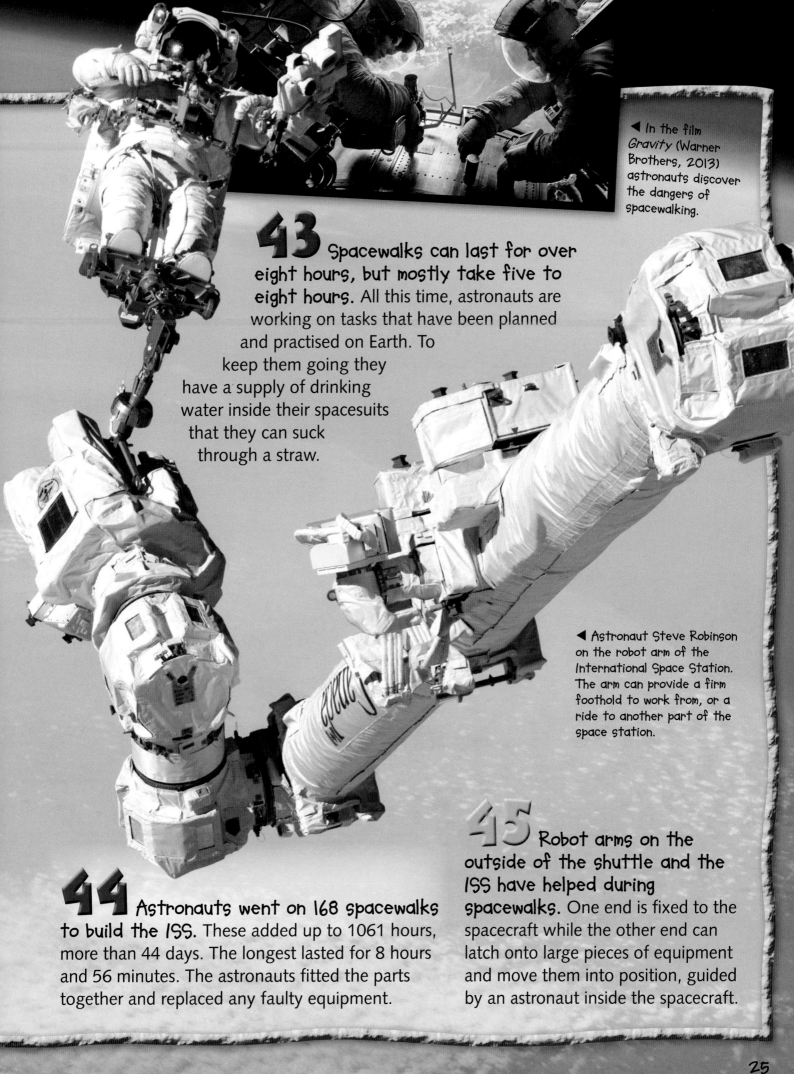

◀ In the film *Gravity* (Warner Brothers, 2013) astronauts discover the dangers of spacewalking.

43 Spacewalks can last for over eight hours, but mostly take five to eight hours. All this time, astronauts are working on tasks that have been planned and practised on Earth. To keep them going they have a supply of drinking water inside their spacesuits that they can suck through a straw.

◀ Astronaut Steve Robinson on the robot arm of the International Space Station. The arm can provide a firm foothold to work from, or a ride to another part of the space station.

44 Astronauts went on 168 spacewalks to build the ISS. These added up to 1061 hours, more than 44 days. The longest lasted for 8 hours and 56 minutes. The astronauts fitted the parts together and replaced any faulty equipment.

45 Robot arms on the outside of the shuttle and the ISS have helped during spacewalks. One end is fixed to the spacecraft while the other end can latch onto large pieces of equipment and move them into position, guided by an astronaut inside the spacecraft.

Living in space

46 The first thing you would notice on a spaceflight is that everything floats. This is called weightlessness. Spacecraft have footholds and straps to keep the astronauts in place while they are working or eating. Everything they use – notebooks, tools, cutlery, toiletries – must be fixed down or they would float away.

▼ Astronauts eating a meal from packets strapped to a table. They use spoons to eat the soft food.

47 All the food on the ISS is brought up from Earth. A lot is dried to save weight, even the drinks. There is no refrigerator so the food is sealed in packets or cans to stop it going off. The astronauts add water to the packet and shake before eating. They drink through a straw from a closed pack because liquids would float out of an open cup.

▼ 1. Wetting hair with drops of water.

▼ 2. Rubbing shampoo through hair.

▲ 3. Combing out clean hair.

▼ Squeezing toothpaste gently onto toothbrush.
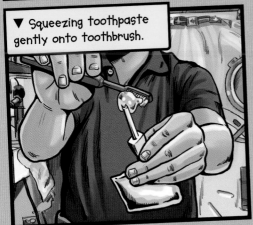

48 **The ISS has no shower.** Astronauts keep clean by washing with a soapy flannel. There is a limited supply of water because it must all be brought up from Earth, so they wash their hair with a special shampoo that doesn't need to be rinsed out. They also have edible toothpaste that they can swallow after brushing their teeth to avoid rinsing and spitting.

49 **When astronauts sleep they must strap themselves down so they don't float around and bump into things.** They usually sleep in sleeping bags fixed to a wall. There are small cabins in the ISS with just enough room for one astronaut in a sleeping bag. Some astronauts use sleep masks and earplugs to block out the noise and light.

▶ Many astronauts find it difficult to sleep soundly in space.

▼ Astronauts fasten themselves on to the toilet so they don't float off.

50 **You cannot flush a toilet with water in space.** Instead, air is used to suck the waste away from the astronauts' bodies. Urine is collected through a tube and cleaned, then the clean water is used again for drinking. All the water on the ISS is cleaned and recycled. The air is recirculated, removing the carbon dioxide breathed out by the astronauts and adding fresh oxygen.

Space stations

51 A space station provides a home in space where astronauts can live and work for months at a time. So far, space stations have all orbited Earth just a few hundred kilometres above its surface. The first space station to be launched was the Russian *Salyut 1* in 1971.

▼ The first module of the ISS was launched in 1998. Astronauts from 14 different countries have stayed in it since.

Canadarm2 robot arm

P1 truss segment

Airlock

52 Modern space stations are built in space. The first one to be built in this way was called *Mir*. It took ten years, from 1986 to 1996, to assemble its six modules. The ISS is four times bigger, and took more than 115 space flights and over ten years to build.

Soyuz

Space Shuttle

▲ The US Space Shuttle *Atlantis* docked with the Russian *Mir* space station in July 1995.

53 The ISS is over 100 metres long, about the length of an American football field. The space occupied by the astronauts is as big as a five bedroomed house, and has two bathrooms and a gym. It weighs about 450,000 kilograms – as much as 320 cars. Six astronauts make up a full crew. There have been people living on board the ISS since November 2000.

54 The electricity to run the ISS comes from the Sun. Eight huge pairs of solar panels, covered with solar cells, change sunlight into electricity. Each pair is about 35 metres long and 11.6 metres wide. Two panels end to end would stretch the width of an American football field. Altogether they make the 75 to 90 kilowatts of power needed to keep the ISS running. The panels twist round to face the Sun so they can make more electricity.

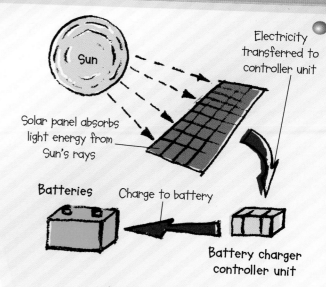

Sun

Electricity transferred to controller unit

Solar panel absorbs light energy from Sun's rays

Batteries

Charge to battery

Battery charger controller unit

▲ Batteries provide power when the ISS is in the Earth's shadow.

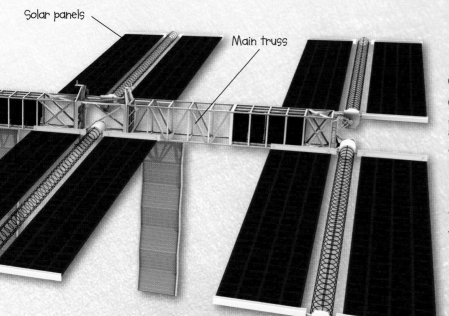

Solar panels

Main truss

55 The basic structure of the ISS is a long beam called a truss that holds the parts together. Attached to it are modules where the astronauts live and work, linked together by nodes. There are docking ports where visiting spacecraft lock on. This is also where supplies are unloaded and astronauts enter.

SPOT THE ISS

The ISS orbits Earth every 90 minutes, and can often be seen in a clear sky just before dawn or just after sunset. It looks like a bright star moving slowly across the sky. The website spotthestation.nasa.gov/sightings will tell you when and where to see it. Enter your country and city to find dates, times, which direction and how high to look in the sky.

56 Astronauts currently travel to and from the space station in a Russian Soyuz spacecraft. Supplies are also brought up to the space station on regular ferries without crews. Russia, Europe and Japan, as well as two private companies, have all launched unmanned supply spacecraft to the ISS.

Space tourists

57 A few very rich people have already paid for a trip into space. The first space tourist was an American called Dennis Tito, who flew to the International Space Station in a Soyuz spacecraft in 2001. His trip lasted for 8 days and cost $20 million.

▲ Cosmonaut Talgat Musabayev (right) helps Dennis Tito get used to weightlessness on his trip to the ISS.

58 Several private companies are now building space planes to take people on short flights into space. *SpaceShipTwo* is one space plane now being tested. It will not go into orbit, but will take six passengers into space for a short time before returning them to Earth.

▼ *SpaceShipTwo* is launched by a special aircraft called *White Knight Two*, which carries it to a height of 15 kilometres above Earth.

▼ The cost of a stay in a future space hotel would be enormous — millions of dollars.

59 In the future, space hotels could be built in orbit. These would be similar to a space station, but for visiting tourists instead of working astronauts. One company called Bigelow Aerospace has already launched inflatable spacecraft that could be built into a hotel, but none that people could live in.

▼ A space station from the science fiction film *Elysium* (TriStar Pictures, 2013).

60 Other companies have suggested offering private space flights to land on the Moon, but one trip would cost billions of dollars. A cheaper option would be to fly in a huge loop around the Moon and back to Earth without landing. The passengers would get a close-up view of the Moon's surface, and would see the far side that cannot be seen from Earth.

I DON'T BELIEVE IT!
One space tourist has paid for two trips to the ISS. In 2007 Charles Simonyi spent 15 days in space, and enjoyed it so much he paid for a second visit in 2009, for another 14 days.

Journey to the Moon

▲ A Saturn V rocket launches the Apollo Command Module with three astronauts inside on their journey to the Moon.

61 Only twelve people have ever set foot on the Moon, and it all happened over 40 years ago. Six Apollo missions landed astronauts on the Moon over three years. The first was *Apollo 11* in July 1969 and the last was *Apollo 17* in December 1972.

62 The Saturn V rocket launched the Apollo spacecraft towards the Moon. It was the most powerful rocket ever to fly successfully. When it was full of fuel, ready for lift-off, it weighed 2.8 million kilograms – about as much as 400 elephants. It had three stages and was 111 metres tall – about as high as a 36-storey building.

63 The journey to the Moon took three days. Three astronauts travelled inside the Apollo Command Module. It was just big enough for the astronauts to move around, with about as much room inside as an estate car. It was perched on top of the Saturn V rocket for lift-off with the Lunar Module, which the astronauts later used to land on the surface.

▼ After the spacecraft was released from the rocket, the Command and Service Module docked with the Lunar Module for the journey to the Moon.

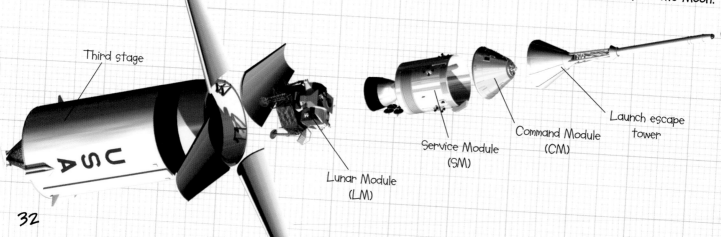

Third stage

Lunar Module (LM)

Service Module (SM)

Command Module (CM)

Launch escape tower

64 When they arrived, two of the astronauts entered the Lunar Module, which then flew down to land on the surface. The third astronaut stayed in the Command Module orbiting the Moon. At the end of the mission, the Lunar Module took off and docked with the Command Module. The astronauts travelled back in the Command Module, leaving the Lunar Module to crash into the Moon.

▶ The Apollo Lunar Module used its engine to land gently on the Moon.

I DON'T BELIEVE IT!

When the first astronauts returned to Earth from the Moon, they had to stay in quarantine for three weeks in case they had brought back any dangerous bugs that could affect people on Earth.

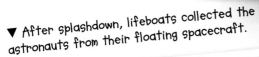
▼ After splashdown, lifeboats collected the astronauts from their floating spacecraft.

65 When it reached Earth, the Command Module with the astronauts inside flew back into the atmosphere. Large parachutes opened to slow it down as it fell towards the ground. It splashed down in the sea for a soft landing. Helicopters transported the astronauts and their spacecraft to a waiting recovery ship. They were then carried safely to land.

Exploring the Moon

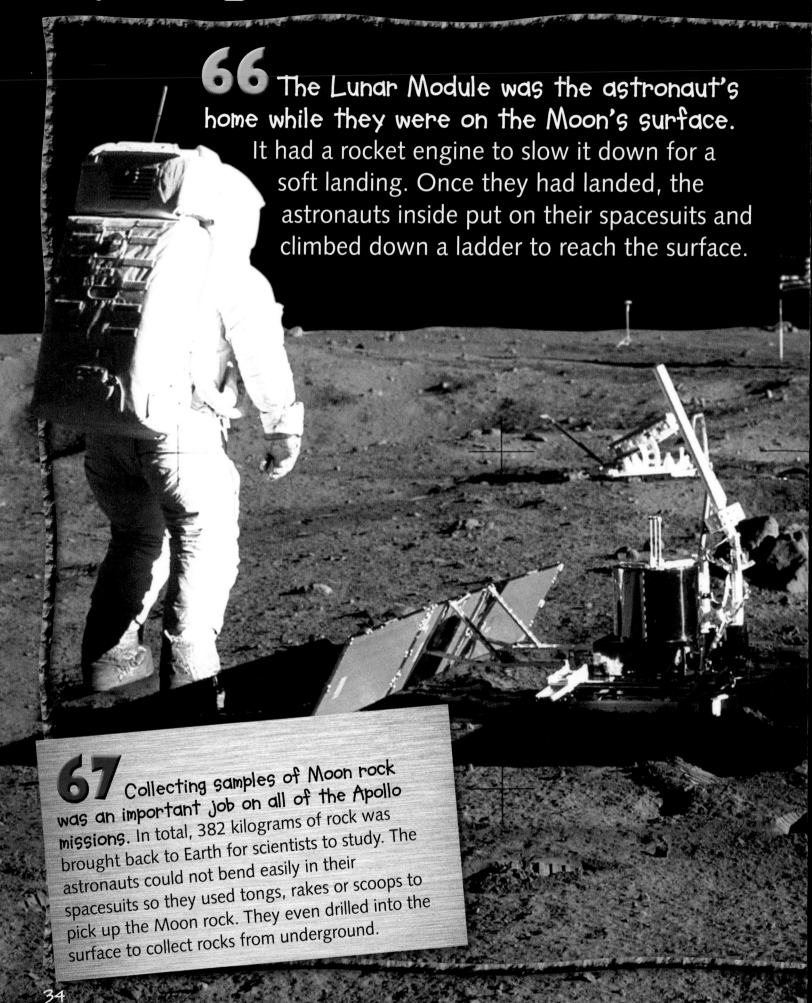

66 The Lunar Module was the astronaut's home while they were on the Moon's surface. It had a rocket engine to slow it down for a soft landing. Once they had landed, the astronauts inside put on their spacesuits and climbed down a ladder to reach the surface.

67 Collecting samples of Moon rock was an important job on all of the Apollo missions. In total, 382 kilograms of rock was brought back to Earth for scientists to study. The astronauts could not bend easily in their spacesuits so they used tongs, rakes or scoops to pick up the Moon rock. They even drilled into the surface to collect rocks from underground.

► Buzz Aldrin sets up experiments near the Lunar Module during the *Apollo 11* mission.

69 On the Moon the astronauts had to wear very bulky spacesuits for protection. On Earth these were very heavy, weighing 82 kilograms, similar to carrying another person around. But on the Moon the pull of gravity is much lower, and so they only weighed 14 kilograms.

70 On the last three Apollo missions, the astronauts had a lunar rover. This was an electric four-wheeled buggy about the size of a small car. It had two seats and room to carry Moon rock back to base. The astronauts used a joystick to drive it. The rover's maximum speed was only around 18 kilometres an hour, but it let the astronauts explore much further.

68 Each of the Apollo missions left experiments on the Moon. These included a mirror, used to bounce a beam of laser light back to Earth to accurately measure the distance. Others listened for moon quakes and monitored radiation. All the information was sent back to Earth as radio signals. Some of the experiments still work today.

HOW MUCH WOULD YOU WEIGH ON THE MOON?

You will need:
a set of bathroom scales

Weigh yourself on the scales and make a note of your weight. Divide it by six. This is what you would weigh on the Moon. Find something that weighs this amount when you put it on the scales – that's how light you would feel on the Moon.

Satellites at work

71 As well as the ISS, hundreds of satellites constantly orbit Earth. Many are in an orbit called geostationary orbit, 35,786 kilometres above Earth. These circle at the same rate as Earth spins. This means that they stay above the same point on Earth, so aerials on the ground do not have to move to catch their signals.

▲ Over half a million pieces of space junk also orbit Earth, making space travel even more dangerous.

Solar panels turn to face Sun

Solar panels provide power

◄ Aerials on *Intelsat* communications satellites relay radio signals from one part of the world to another.

Satellite points down to Earth

Aerials send and receive radio signals

72 Communications satellites send radio signals carrying telephone conversations and TV programmes all around the world. Pictures of news and events from distant countries travel up to a satellite in space then back down to Earth to get to your TV. Satellites also let us talk on the phone to people thousands of miles away.

QUIZ

1. What kind of signals do communications satellites send?
2. How high above Earth is geostationary orbit?
3. Which kind of satellite watches cloud movements and measures temperatures?

Answers:
1. Radio signals
2. 35,786 kilometres
3. A meteorological or weather satellite

73 Navigation satellites can tell you where you are, how fast you are moving and direct you to where you are going. The Global Positioning System (GPS) has around 30 satellites circling Earth. Satnav equipment picks up signals from several satellites and uses the information to work out your position and speed.

▶ Each *Navstar* navigation satellite circles Earth twice every day, so that signals from at least four satellites are available everywhere on Earth.

74 Meteorological satellites help forecasters predict the weather. They look at Earth's atmosphere, watching cloud movements and measuring land and sea temperatures. The information is sent to huge computers, which use it to calculate weather forecasts.

▼ *Solar and Heliospheric Observatory (SOHO)* orbits between Earth and the Sun to give early warning of Sun storms.

75 Satellites looking down from space can spot pollution on Earth. They can also track wild animals and icebergs, and spot forest fires. Astronomical satellites look out into space to discover planets around distant stars, and find out what the Universe was like billions of years ago. Some watch the Sun for storms that could send dangerous bursts of radiation towards Earth.

Long distance space travel

76 A journey through space must be planned very carefully. Everything in space is moving very fast, so when launching a spacecraft mission planners have to decide which way to send it to make sure it doesn't miss its target.

▶ When *Voyager 2* flew by Jupiter in 1979 it used the giant planet's gravity to pick up speed and change direction for its rendezvous with Saturn.

Jupiter

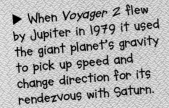

Voyager 2

▲ *Voyager 2* captured close up pictures of the planet Neptune as it flew past in 1989.

77 Spacecraft can save fuel on a journey by swinging around a planet to gain speed. This is called a sling shot or gravity assist, because it uses the gravity of the planet to propel it on its way much faster. The *Voyager 2* space probe flew past the four furthest planets from the Sun – Jupiter, Saturn, Uranus and Neptune. At each of these it gained enough speed to reach the next.

I DON'T BELIEVE IT!

Launched in 1977, the *Voyager 1* space probe has now reached the edge of the Solar System – about 19 billion kilometres away. It is still sending back information, but its signals take over 16 hours to reach Earth.

78 Ion engines can gradually provide extra speed over the vast distances in space. They use magnets to send a stream of tiny electrical particles called ions out of the engine, pushing the spacecraft forwards. They only provide a very tiny thrust (push) but they can keep going, unlike rocket engines, which run out of fuel. In the future, they may help spacecraft reach the outer Solar System.

◄ The *SMART-1* spacecraft used ion engines on its flight to the Moon in 2003.

79 Solar sails may also be used to push spacecraft along in the future. They are huge sheets of very thin, light material that are pushed along by sunlight. Spacecraft with solar sails would be launched by a rocket, then the sail would unfold. The sunlight gives a weak but constant push to the sail, which gradually gains speed. In 2010 Japan launched the first solar sailing spacecraft called *IKAROS*.

▼ In the future, huge solar sails like this could propel spacecraft through space.

80 Radio signals take a long time to travel to and from spacecraft far out in space. When controllers on Earth send instructions to a spacecraft exploring Mars, they may arrive up to 20 minutes later. This is much too late to stop a rover colliding with a rock, so many spacecraft are programmed to operate without instructions from Earth.

81 Space probes are unmanned craft that travel through space to explore planets, moons, asteroids and comets. Probes have investigated all the planets in our Solar System. They carry instruments and cameras to measure temperatures, radiation and magnetism.

I DON'T BELIEVE IT!

Aerogel is an extremely light material, mostly made up of empty space. In 2004 the *Stardust* probe used aerogel to collect particles of comet dust as it could trap the tiny particles without damaging them.

▼ After a seven year journey to Saturn the *Cassini* probe dropped a smaller probe onto Saturn's moon Titan.

82 Some probes fly close to their target but do not stop. They collect pictures and information, then fly on. Others go into orbit around it. They can send back pictures of the whole surface and watch for changes. For a really close look, some spacecraft actually land on their target. They can find out what the surface is made of around their landing site.

▼ The *Curiosity* rover moves very slowly, covering only about 30 metres in an hour.

83 The *Curiosity* rover is a robot spacecraft that is currently exploring the planet Mars. It is a six-wheeled rover about the size of a car that moves slowly across the dusty surface, steering to avoid any large rocks. It takes close-up pictures of the soil and rocks, and can drill into the rocks and test them to see what they are made of.

84 Several space probes have been sent out to intercept comets. *Giotto* was the first probe to send back pictures of a comet's nucleus, which cannot be seen from Earth. It photographed Halley's comet in 1986. The *Stardust* probe collected tiny dust particles from comet Wild 2's huge glowing tail in 2004. It flew back to Earth and delivered a capsule containing the samples, before continuing on to begin a new mission.

85 Asteroids (chunks of rock that orbit the Sun between the planets Mars and Jupiter) are also a target for space probes. *Hayabusa* is a Japanese probe that landed on a small asteroid called Itokawa in 2005. It brought a sample of asteroid dust back to Earth for scientists to study.

▶ *Giotto* flew into the tail of Halley's comet to get close-up pictures of the nucleus.

▲ The nucleus of Halley's comet was tiny and very dark.

A visit to Mars?

86 The next possible place for astronauts to visit is Mars. There have been plans to send people to Mars even before the first Moon landing, although it would be a very dangerous and expensive mission. People could not survive on Mars without spacesuits and they would need protection from radiation and the extreme cold.

► Astronauts on a visit to Mars could use a rover to explore Mars' rocky surface and as a base to live in.

Astronauts might not wear spacesuits inside the rover

87 It would take six to nine months to travel to Mars, and the same for the trip back. One mission that has been suggested would fly two people to Mars, not to land, but to go around it and back to Earth. The trip would take nearly 17 months, and the crew would spend all of this time inside their spacecraft. If astronauts landed on Mars, they could be away from Earth for two years or more.

VISAS 10   VISAS 11

QUIZ
1. Is there water on Mars?
2. How long would a round trip to Mars take?
3. Could astronauts breathe the air on Mars?

does not contain oxygen
No, the air on

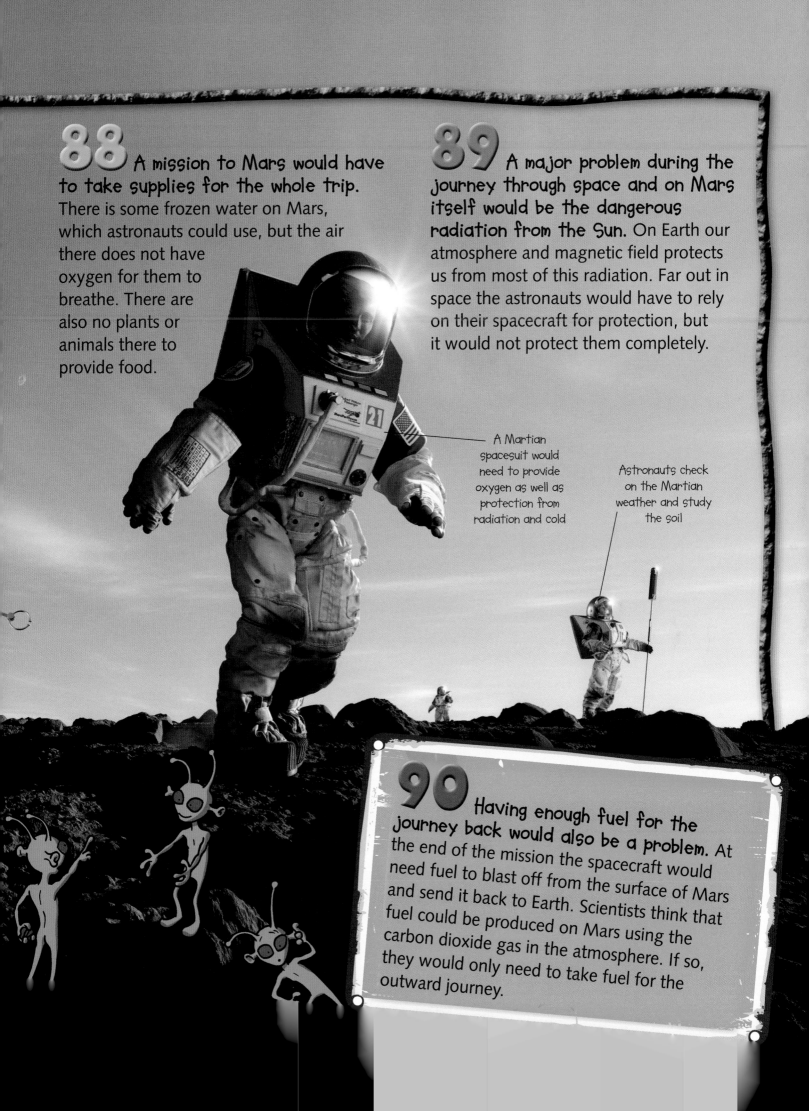

88 A mission to Mars would have to take supplies for the whole trip. There is some frozen water on Mars, which astronauts could use, but the air there does not have oxygen for them to breathe. There are also no plants or animals there to provide food.

89 A major problem during the journey through space and on Mars itself would be the dangerous radiation from the Sun. On Earth our atmosphere and magnetic field protects us from most of this radiation. Far out in space the astronauts would have to rely on their spacecraft for protection, but it would not protect them completely.

A Martian spacesuit would need to provide oxygen as well as protection from radiation and cold

Astronauts check on the Martian weather and study the soil

90 Having enough fuel for the journey back would also be a problem. At the end of the mission the spacecraft would need fuel to blast off from the surface of Mars and send it back to Earth. Scientists think that fuel could be produced on Mars using the carbon dioxide gas in the atmosphere. If so, they would only need to take fuel for the outward journey.

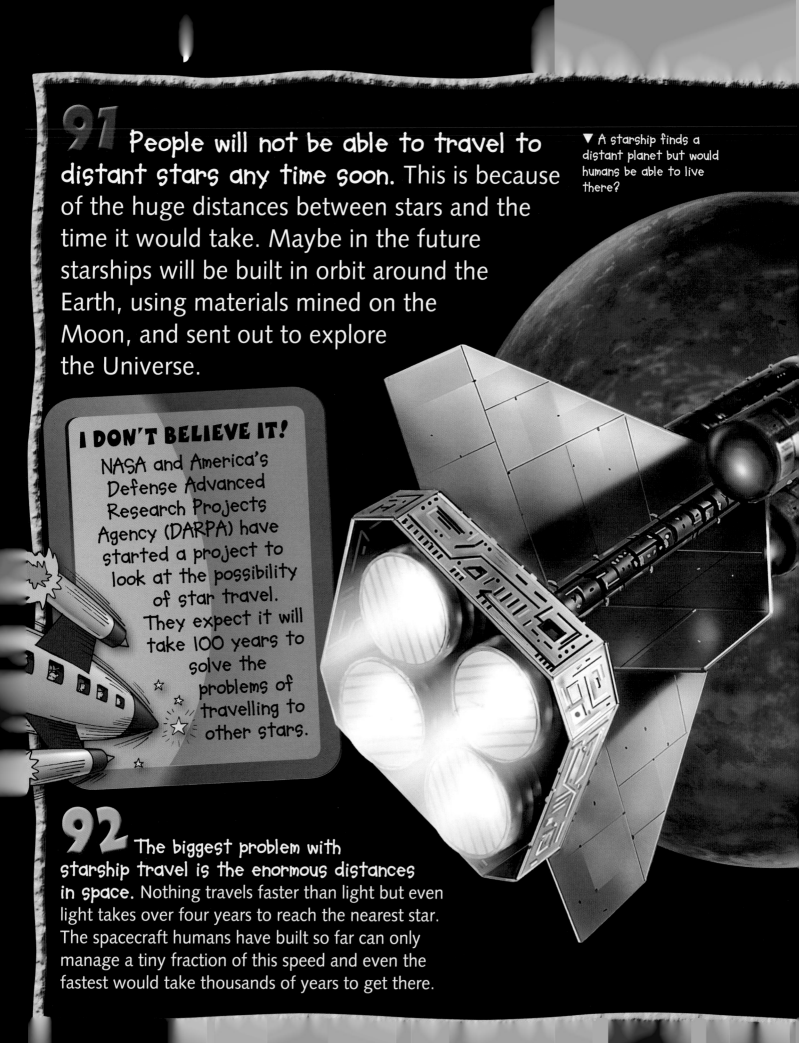

91 **People will not be able to travel to distant stars any time soon.** This is because of the huge distances between stars and the time it would take. Maybe in the future starships will be built in orbit around the Earth, using materials mined on the Moon, and sent out to explore the Universe.

▼ A starship finds a distant planet but would humans be able to live there?

I DON'T BELIEVE IT!

NASA and America's Defense Advanced Research Projects Agency (DARPA) have started a project to look at the possibility of star travel. They expect it will take 100 years to solve the problems of travelling to other stars.

92 **The biggest problem with starship travel is the enormous distances in space.** Nothing travels faster than light but even light takes over four years to reach the nearest star. The spacecraft humans have built so far can only manage a tiny fraction of this speed and even the fastest would take thousands of years to get there.

93 People have suggested that the human crew of a starship could go into hibernation for the journey by lowering their temperature to below freezing. However, we do not know if they would survive and wake up at the end of the journey. Some frogs and tiny microscopic creatures can survive being frozen but it has not been tried with humans.

▲ If a human space crew was put into 'hibernation' for a journey to a distant star, computers would pilot the starship and revive them after the long journey.

94 A huge starship that is completely self-sufficient is called an 'interstellar ark'. It would be big enough to grow food for everyone on board and recycle the air and water, just like an island in space. It would spin slowly to give the crew the feeling of gravity. People would live their whole lives and have children and grandchildren during the voyage. Eventually the descendants of the original crew would arrive at their destination.

▼ In the film *Avatar* (20th Century Fox, 2009), the aliens are 3 metres tall and have blue skin.

95 Nobody knows what these space travellers would find if they reached another world. They would hope to find another planet like Earth where they could live. However, other planets may not have the water and oxygen that humans need to survive. If they did find a planet that humans could live on it might already have inhabitants who would not welcome a starship full of people, all of whom would seem like aliens to them.

Space travel in books and films

96 Travelling through space to distant stars and galaxies is a common theme in science fiction. Before rockets were invented, authors imagined materials and technology that could overcome gravity and send people into space. In his 1865 story, *From the Earth to the Moon*, Jules Verne used a giant cannon to shoot space travellers to the Moon.

▶ The starship *Enterprise* in *Star Trek* had 'warp drive' — a propulsion system that allowed it to travel faster than light.

97 Stories would not be very exciting if spaceships took thousands of years to travel between stars. Instead, authors invent special devices to allow them to travel faster than light. Films like *Star Wars* use 'Hyperspace' – highways through space where spaceships can travel faster than light.

98 Weightlessness is not always a problem for astronauts in films. They walk around in their spaceships as though on Earth. Starships in films are also very spacious inside with plenty of room for astronauts to move about. It looks very different from the way the real astronauts live on the International Space Station.

99 Time travel is also common in science fiction. In these stories people do not travel through space, they go back or forward in time using an imaginary time machine or an invisible gateway in time. In H.G.Wells' book, *The Time Machine*, the traveller goes thousands of years into the future. In the *Doctor Who* TV series the time machine, the Tardis, can travel through time and space.

100 Many stories feature aliens travelling through outer space to visit Earth. Some are friendly – in the film *E.T. The Extra-Terrestrial* (Universal Pictures, 1982) a young alien just wants to go home to his own world. Others are more threatening, like the attacking spaceships in the film *Independence Day* (20th Century Fox, 1996).

▶ E.T., a young space traveller visiting Earth, has special powers that can make bicycles fly through the air.

QUIZ
1. Which starship had warp drive to travel faster than light?
2. What is the name of Doctor Who's time machine?
3. In which story are people shot to the Moon in a giant cannon?

Answers:
1. The starship Enterprise
2. The Tardis 3. From the Earth to the Moon by Jules Verne

Index

Page numbers in **bold** refer
to main entries, those in *italics* refer to
illustrations.